BUILDING BY DESIGN

ENGINEERING
AT&T STADIUM

BY BARBARA LOWELL

CONTENT CONSULTANT
Steven C. Maki
Steven Maki Consulting PLCC

Core Library

Cover image: AT&T Stadium is one of the NFL's newest and most popular stadiums.

An Imprint of Abdo Publishing
abdopublishing.com

abdopublishing.com

Published by Abdo Publishing, a division of ABDO, PO Box 398166, Minneapolis, Minnesota 55439. Copyright © 2018 by Abdo Consulting Group, Inc. International copyrights reserved in all countries. No part of this book may be reproduced in any form without written permission from the publisher. Core Library™ is a trademark and logo of Abdo Publishing.

Printed in the United States of America, North Mankato, Minnesota
042017
092017

Cover Photo: Steve Debenport/iStockphoto
Interior Photos: Steve Debenport/iStockphoto, 1, 20, 45; Andrew Dieb/Icon Sportswire, 4–5, 43; Matthew Pearce/Icon Sportswire, 6; Evan Agostini/Invision/AP Images, 8; Tony Gutierrez/ AP Images, 10; Ric Tapia/AP Images, 12–13, 30–31; Shutterstock Images, 15; James D. Smith/AP Images, 16, 38–39; Red Line Editorial, 19; Chris Graythen/Getty Images Sport/Getty Images, 22–23; David Pellerin/AP Images, 25; Andrey Krav/iStockphoto, 27 (top left); Mike Fuentes/Bloomberg/ Getty Images, 27 (bottom); iStockphoto, 27 (top right), 34–35; Dr. Scott M. Lieberman/AP Images, 28; Ronald Martinez/Getty Images Sport/Getty Images, 37

Editor: Heidi Schoof
Imprint Designer: Maggie Villaume
Series Design Direction: Laura Polzin

Publisher's Cataloging-in-Publication Data

Names: Lowell, Barbara, author.
Title: Engineering AT&T Stadium / by Barbara Lowell.
Description: Minneapolis, MN : Abdo Publishing, 2018. | Series: Building by design | Includes bibliographical references and index.
Identifiers: LCCN 2017930238 | ISBN 9781532111617 (lib. bdg.) | ISBN 9781680789461 (ebook)
Subjects: LCSH: Structural engineering--Miscellanea--Juvenile literature. | Stadiums--Design and construction--Juvenile literature. | Buildings, structures, etc.--Juvenile literature. | Buildings--Miscellanea--Juvenile literature.
Classification: DDC 624--dc23
LC record available at http://lccn.loc.gov/2017930238

CONTENTS

A NEW HOME FOR THE DALLAS COWBOYS

O n a sunny fall day, more than 80,000 football fans stream into AT&T Stadium in Arlington, Texas. It is the home of the Dallas Cowboys. Fans walk by colorful murals painted on the walls. They see art pieces made of glass, stainless steel, and mirrors. And they sit in seats specially designed to be comfortable.

Light shines on the field from the open retractable roof and end zone doors.

Dallas Cowboys fans fill the sunlit AT&T Stadium on game days throughout the season.

Cowboys star Ezekiel Elliot catches a pass in a 2016 game.

The quarterback takes the snap and drops back. He circles to his left as if he is going to run the ball down the field. Defenders rush toward him. The quarterback scans to the left and right, looking for an open receiver. Fans watch as he spots one down the field. He throws the football. The pass is in the air. The receiver jumps, catches the ball, and races into the end zone for a touchdown.

Cowboys fans cheer. They watch a replay of the touchdown on the giant video screen high above the field. No one in the stadium missed a second of the action. Three thousand televisions are scattered throughout AT&T Stadium. Cowboys fans can even watch the game on huge screens outside the stadium.

IDEAS FOR THE STADIUM

Jerry Jones is the Dallas Cowboys' owner. For nearly a decade before construction began in 2006, he and his family gathered ideas for AT&T Stadium's design. They looked all over the world for inspiration. They dreamed of building

PERSPECTIVES

SEARCHING FOR IDEAS

The Jones family found inspiration for their new stadium in many places. They visited stadiums, arenas, museums, and airports around the world. They examined both huge structures and tiny details. Then they worked with architects and engineers to bring these features to the Cowboys' new stadium.

Jerry, *right*, and Eugenia Jones and their three adult children all hold executive roles in the Cowboys organization.

a sleek, modern stadium, open all year. The new home of the Dallas Cowboys would be more than a National Football League (NFL) stadium. College football, soccer, basketball, concerts, and special events would be played there, too.

The Jones family wanted the stadium to be immense. It would seat 80,000 people at Cowboys home games. It could be expanded to hold 100,000 people for special events, such as the Super Bowl.

SKY MIRROR

Art is an important part of AT&T Stadium. One piece of art there is called the Sky Mirror. This circular, stainless-steel mirror stands at the east entrance. It is 35 feet (10.7 m) in diameter. Its front curves and tilts toward the sky. The mirror reflects the sky's color and clouds. It even reflects passing airplanes. Its back is also a mirror, so fans can see themselves.

The family wanted the stadium to be enclosed and air conditioned. At the same time, they wanted it to feel like an open stadium, with lots of light shining in. The stadium would have a curved roof that opened and closed. This would keep the hole-in-the-roof design of Texas Stadium, the Cowboys' old stadium. The Jones family also wanted every fan to have a great view of

Artist Anish Kapoor's Sky Mirror had temporary homes in New York and London, England, before finding a permanent spot on the east plaza of AT&T Stadium.

the field and see the action up close on video screens.

All these ideas presented challenges. It was up to engineers to make the ideas work.

STRAIGHT TO THE
SOURCE

An article in *Building Design+Construction* magazine details the process the Jones family went through when imagining the new stadium:

> *The Jones family spent many hours studying sporting venues and other large structures worldwide. "It would be hard to single out any one structure, because we learned from so many, be it a visual design element or a concept on space layout," [Jerry] Jones explained. "We spent a great deal of time studying the architecture of buildings across the country as well as Europe, Asia and Australia. And we didn't just focus on stadiums; we studied hotels, office towers, museums, and other public buildings as well. . . ." "Jerry Jones painted a vision of the stadium and the architects and engineers worked closely with him and the Jones family developing a design," said Mark Williams, project director.*

Source: Liz Moucka. "Dallas Cowboys Stadium." *Building Design+Construction*. Building Design+Construction, April 21, 2008. Web. Accessed February 24, 2017.

Consider Your Audience

Rewrite the passage as a blog post for your friends. How is your post different from the passage? How is it similar?

DESIGNING SOLUTIONS

A major goal for AT&T Stadium was to build an enclosed stadium that feels like an open one. The retractable roof design helps. And even when the roof is closed, its translucent surface lets light in. The addition of giant doors at both end zones opened the stadium to the outdoors. When the doors are closed, light shines through their clear glass.

Glass walls and a window near the top of the stadium were designed to bring in even more light. The window wraps around the building just below the roofline.

AT&T Stadium was designed to be a vast, open space, flooded with natural light.

GLASS WALLS

The glass walls of AT&T Stadium change color with the changing color of the sky. The colors range from blue to silver to gray. These are the colors of the Dallas Cowboys' uniforms. At night, the glass walls glow, reflecting the lights inside the stadium.

Inside the glass walls are tiny dots. Light shines in around them. The bottom of the glass wall has many more dots than the top. This means more light shines in at the top of the walls than at the bottom. All these ideas worked together to give Cowboys fans an outdoor stadium experience in an indoor stadium.

A GREAT VIEW

Another goal was to give every football fan a great view of the field. In many stadiums, columns support the roof. But columns prevent some fans from seeing the field clearly. AT&T Stadium's engineers designed two enormous arches rising high above the playing field. They support the roof so that columns aren't needed. Everyone in the stadium can see the football field.

The glass walls of the stadium both reflect its surroundings and invite the outdoors in, with 360-degree views inside and out.

Arches have been used in construction since ancient times. The curved design of an arch is strong. It transfers the weight it supports down its sides and into the ground. Arches can hold tremendous amounts of weight.

AT&T Stadium's arches also support the 1.2-million-pound (544,800-kg) video scoreboard. It hangs 90 feet (27.4 m) above the playing field. Its four screens tilt down toward the seats. The two screens on the long side of the field measure 160 feet (49 m) wide

and 72 feet (22 m) tall. The football players look larger than life. The giant scoreboard gives every Cowboys fan a great way to watch the football action up close.

EXPANDABLE SEATING AND REMOVABLE FIELDS

The stadium's designers wanted to be able to add more seats for special events. In most stadiums, the seats are bolted into concrete. They cannot be moved. In AT&T Stadium, the solution was a rail design. The seats are attached to a metal rail and can be pushed closer together. Extra seats can be added to each row. Areas for standing room are another part of the design.

NFL, college football, and soccer teams play on different fields. AT&T Stadium needed three separate fields to hold all these games. Three fields of artificial grass were designed. Each field can be removed and replaced with one of the other two fields.

The giant video scoreboard dwarfs the players on the field while making every spectator part of the action.

WEATHER SOLUTIONS

Arlington experiences some of the harshest weather on Earth. It is located in Tornado Alley. Severe storms, high winds, and tornadoes occur in this region of the United States. Arlington also experiences extremes in temperature. The temperature can reach more than 100 degrees Fahrenheit (38°C) in the summer. Winters can be cold, with ice and snowstorms. Engineers found ways to protect the stadium and keep the people inside comfortable.

In hot weather, the roof and end zone doors are closed.

STADIUMS IN TORNADO ALLEY

CANADA

Memorial Stadium (University of Nebraska–Lincoln)

Bill Snyder Family Football Stadium

University of Kansas Memorial Stadium

Boone Pickens Stadium

Gaylord Family Oklahoma Memorial Stadium

PACIFIC
OCEAN

Cotton Bowl

AT&T Stadium

MEXICO

GULF OF
MEXICO

ATLANTIC
OCEAN

Tornado Alley

N
W E
S

Find the professional and college football stadiums located in Tornado Alley. What can people living in these areas learn from the engineers who worked on AT&T Stadium?

The stadium is air conditioned. To help keep it cool, a curved roof was chosen. Cold air is denser than hot air. Hot air rises, while cold air stays closer to the ground. The large, curved roof traps hot air above. The cool air stays in the seating area.

The stadium's color also plays a part in keeping fans comfortable. A light gray color was chosen for the

An aerial view of AT&T Stadium shows the retractable roof panels and the tracks on which they open and close.

stadium's roof. It reflects the sun's rays and helps keep the inside of the stadium at 78 degrees Fahrenheit (25.5°C).

A five-layer covering shields the roof from wind and storms. The bottom layer helps protect the roof from high winds. The top layer is waterproof. Rain, snow, and ice slide off the roof. Engineers tested the materials in a wind tunnel. The stadium's roof can withstand winds up to 115 miles per hour (185 km/h).

A ROOF THAT OPENS AND CLOSES

The open roof had to close to protect people inside the stadium from the weather. Two huge roof panels were designed to fit over the opening. They meet above the

50-yard line. Opening and closing the panels on a flat roof would work easily. AT&T Stadium's steep, curving roof presented a problem.

Engineers designed a rack-and-pinion system. A pinion is a toothed gear wheel. A rack is a toothed gear bar. The pinion moves along the rack when the roof opens or closes. Its gear teeth fit into the rack's gear teeth. This prevents the panels from sliding off the roof. The roof panels are operated by 128 motors. Since gravity helps to open the panels, the motors work mostly as brakes. The motors pull the panels up when the roof closes. Opening or closing the roof takes 12 minutes.

EXPLORE ONLINE

Chapter Two mentions the enormous video scoreboard in AT&T Stadium. Visit the website below to learn more about the Dallas Cowboys' scoreboard. How is the information similar to Chapter Two? How is it different? What new information did you learn?

HOW THE DALLAS COWBOYS SCOREBOARD WORKS

abdocorelibrary.com/engineering-att-stadium

CHAPTER
THREE

BUILDING AT&T STADIUM

C onstruction work on AT&T Stadium began in the spring of 2006. Workers dug a huge hole using earthmovers and bulldozers. They created a bowl shape to hold the field and seating areas. The workers built a giant wall around the bowl. The wall prevented dirt and rocks from falling into the seating bowl during construction.

Huge underground columns of concrete and steel support the stadium and the area around it. Once these were in place, workers

Major League Baseball fans had this view of the ongoing stadium construction from nearby Rangers Ballpark in the spring of 2008.

built concrete seating areas, walls, and stairs. Cranes lifted these pieces up in sections and placed them in the seating bowl.

CONSTRUCTING THE ARCHES

AT&T Stadium's two arches are connected to concrete structures called abutments. Part of each abutment sits above the ground, and part is below ground. Construction workers built four abutments, one for each end of the arches. Underneath the abutments are steel cages 70 feet (21 m) tall. Workers built the cages and dropped them underground. They filled the cages with concrete. All the weight of the arches, the roof, and the scoreboard transfers down through the abutments and into the cages. The concrete-filled cages support all this weight.

To begin construction of the arches, steel pivots were fastened to the abutments. The pivots move like door hinges. During hot and cold weather, the metal in the arches expands and contracts. The arches move up

Four concrete abutments support the weight of the stadium's massive arches and its roof.

and down about two feet (0.6 m). The pivots prevent the arches from breaking by moving with them.

Tall steel towers supported the arches during construction. Construction of the first arch began at an abutment. Huge steel pieces called trusses were lifted up by cranes. Each truss was so heavy that extra weight had to be placed on top of the cranes to balance them. Ironworkers bolted the trusses together to form the arch.

When one side of the arch was almost complete, work on the other side began. The last truss, called the keystone piece, fit into the center of the arch. It fit within 0.25 inches (0.64 cm) on each side. With the ends of the arches so far apart, this was an amazing accomplishment. Work on the second arch began when the first arch was finished. It took five months to build each arch.

ROOF CONSTRUCTION

The roof was constructed of steel and covered with a five-layer protective covering. The roof is steep because

COMPARING ARCHES

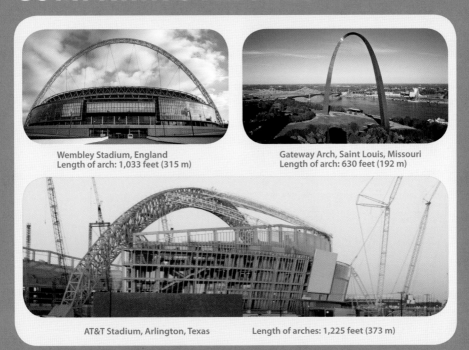

Wembley Stadium, England
Length of arch: 1,033 feet (315 m)

Gateway Arch, Saint Louis, Missouri
Length of arch: 630 feet (192 m)

AT&T Stadium, Arlington, Texas   Length of arches: 1,225 feet (373 m)

Look at the photos of arches at Wembley Stadium in London, England, the Gateway Arch in Saint Louis, Missouri, and AT&T Stadium. How are the arches at AT&T Stadium different from the arch at Wembley Stadium and the Gateway Arch? How are they similar?

it is curved. Anything on top of the roof can easily fall off. Windy conditions made working on the roof even more dangerous. The construction crews were attached to double safety lines. All their equipment had to be bolted down. Every piece of material they used was tied onto the roof as well.

Workers installed the multi-layered roof of AT&T Stadium in the fall of 2008.

The crews attached the roofing layers. They heat-welded the layers together. Crews of workers "broom surfed" to remove air from under the top layer. One worker from each crew stood on the broom while two workers guided it down the roof.

BUILDING AND RAISING THE VIDEO SCOREBOARD

Three construction teams built the video scoreboard frame on the field at the 50-yard line. Crane operators held the steel pieces in place. Welders and ironworkers fitted them together. The frame has ten levels. Each level has a narrow walkway. When the frame was complete, two huge cranes raised it above the field. It hangs from cables attached to the two main arches and two smaller arches.

The four screens are made of LED panels. Cranes lifted each panel into the air. Workers sitting in the scoreboard frame caught the panels and secured them in place.

INSTALLING GLASS DOORS AND WALLS

Seven giant glass doors sit at each end zone. The two outer doors on each end do not move. The five center doors slide to the sides

PERSPECTIVES
RAISING AND LOWERING THE SCOREBOARD

The band U2 played at AT&T Stadium soon after it opened. But the scoreboard presented a problem. The band's stage was too tall to fit under it. A cable drive system was designed. It can raise the video board to 115 feet (35 m) and lower it to 25 feet (7.6 m) above the field. Additional cable drives were added to keep the scoreboard from moving from side to side. On Cowboys game days, the scoreboard stands 90 feet (27.4 m) above the football field.

The enormous video scoreboard is suspended by cables from the main arches and two smaller arches that connect them.

in front of them. It takes 18 minutes to open or close the doors.

The door frames are made of steel. Workers laid them flat on the ground before they were installed. A hinge was attached to the bottom of each door frame. A crane lifted the top of each frame. At first, the crane and the hinge shared the weight of the frame. Once the frame was at a 45-degree angle, the hinge began

to take more of the weight. The hinge took all of the weight once the frame stood upright.

Next, the top of the door frame was attached to rollers. The rollers sit inside a metal track. They allow the doors to slide open or closed. Glass panels were put into each door frame. The end zone doors create an opening 180 feet (55 m) wide.

The outside glass walls are made of 5,071 panels. Each panel fits into a frame made of steel and aluminum. Workers fit the glass panels into the frame. The workers had a challenging job because the frames extend out at an angle. Gravity pulled the panels straight down. The workers had to fight gravity to push each panel into its frame.

THE HEATING AND COOLING SYSTEM

Workers installed an enormous heating and cooling system. Cranes lifted the huge air ducts. Most of the ducts are more than eight feet (2.4 m) in diameter. Ironworkers fastened to safety lines stood on scaffolds hung from the ceiling. The workers had to climb off the scaffolds to reach the highest ducts. They stood 250 feet (76 m) above the stadium floor. They balanced on the tops of steel beams and on the edges of the ducts. The workers fit and bolted the ducts together. They completed almost two miles (3 km) of ductwork.

STRAIGHT TO THE
SOURCE

Author Jeff Sullivan described how parts and processes from all over the world came together to build the massive arches of AT&T Stadium:

Each arch would weigh over 6.5 million pounds [2.95 million kg] and would hold nearly 20 million pounds [90 million Newtons] of thrust, figures that were literally unheard of in a building of this type. . . . The process began at a mill in Luxembourg of all places, the only plant in the world that could produce the strength of steel needed for such a project. The raw steel was shipped to New Orleans, then loaded on a train bound for Oklahoma City, a company there cleaning, cutting, fabricating, and finally painting the massive pieces. Eventually, each section was trucked down to the job site in Arlington, where only then could they finally be connected. In all, the process took 10 months to complete.

Source: Jeff Sullivan. *America's Team: The Official History of the Dallas Cowboys*. San Rafael, CA: Insight Editions, 2010. Print.

Back It Up

Read the passage. What is the author's main point? Write a paragraph to describe the main point. Then write two or three examples the author uses to support the main point.

AN AMAZING STADIUM

Jerry Jones and his family realized their dream. They built an exceptional stadium. AT&T Stadium is recognized around the world. It is known for its giant arches, its retractable roof, and its 60-yard-long (55-m) scoreboard. It is one of the largest stadiums in the world.

The stadium, originally called Cowboys Stadium, opened in the summer of 2009. The phone company AT&T bought naming rights to the stadium in 2013. Having its name on the stadium advertises the company. News reports estimated it spends about $17 million per year for the rights.

AT&T Stadium is easily recognizable by its unique design features.

AT&T Stadium uses modern technology, but it also pays tribute to the team's history. The stadium honors outstanding Dallas Cowboys players of the past. Their names and numbers are on the Ring of Honor. It circles the inside of the stadium at one of the upper levels.

THE AT&T STADIUM SIGNS

When the name of the stadium changed to AT&T Stadium, giant signs were added. An Austin, Texas, sign company made two sets of 43-foot-tall (13-m) letters. Each 11-letter sign says "AT&T STADIUM." The letters traveled by truck to Arlington. It took 46 trips to move all the letters. Every trip created a traffic jam with its oversized loads. The signs were installed on the north and south sides of the dome roof. A crane lifted each letter into place. Workers on the roof secured them. It took 33 hours to complete each sign.

THE FIRST GAMES IN THE NEW STADIUM

The Cowboys played their first football game at the new stadium in August 2009. During the third quarter of the preseason game, the Tennessee Titans punter kicked the football. It hit the new scoreboard, and

Fans arrive for the Cowboys' first regular-season game in the brand-new stadium in September 2009.

the play had to be repeated. The punter kicked the football again. This time he missed the scoreboard. The Cowboys went on to win the game 30–10.

The Cowboys played their first regular-season game on September 20, 2009. More than 105,000 people squeezed into the stadium to watch the Cowboys play the New York Giants. The final score was close, but the Cowboys lost the game 33–31.

German artist Franz Ackermann painted murals directly on the walls of the southwest staircase.

EVENTS

Many championship basketball, soccer, and football games, including the Super Bowl, have been played

at AT&T Stadium. AT&T Stadium hosts many special events, too. They range from music concerts to motorbike races to bull riding. On non-event days, visitors and schoolchildren line up for tours. They explore the enormous stadium from top to bottom.

LIGHTING UP THE STADIUM

A new LED lighting system was added to AT&T Stadium in 2015. The LED lights are bright and use less electricity than older types of light bulbs. The lights shine on the field, producing excellent lighting for television.

THE ART COLLECTION

A dream of the Jones family was to add an art collection to AT&T Stadium. Many people never visit an art museum.

Everyone who visits AT&T Stadium can view the collection. Art pieces are on display inside and outside the stadium.

With AT&T Stadium, the Jones family succeeded in creating an amazing structure. They dreamed big and built an exceptional stadium. For Dallas Cowboys fans, the stadium provides a place to watch thrilling football games. For fans of architecture, it stands as a marvel of modern design, engineering, and construction.

FURTHER EVIDENCE

Chapter Four discusses several of the stadium's incredible architectural features. Visit the website below to read more about the stadium's features and one of the companies that created them. Does the information on this page support facts from Chapter Four? Does it add new information?

UNI-SYSTEMS: COWBOYS STADIUM
abdocorelibrary.com/engineering-att-stadium

FAST FACTS

- Jerry Jones and his family looked for ideas for AT&T Stadium around the world.

- The phone company AT&T bought naming rights to the stadium for approximately $17 million per year.

- AT&T Stadium was designed to hold 100,000 people.

- The stadium's end zone doors and retractable roof make it feel like an open stadium.

- The stadium is supported by underground columns.

- Two immense arches support the roof and the video scoreboard.

- AT&T Stadium's arches are each 1,225 feet (373 m) long.

- The video scoreboard's largest two screens measure 160 feet (49 m) wide and 72 feet (22 m) tall.

- The special roof covering protects the roof from high winds and rain.

- A rack-and-pinion system opens and closes the retractable roof. It prevents the roof panels from sliding off the roof.

- The stadium has three removable playing fields.

STOP AND
THINK

Tell the Tale

Chapter One of this book discusses the Jones family's travels to find ideas for the new stadium. Imagine that you are building a stadium and visiting landmarks to find ideas. Write 200 words about the places you visit. How will these places inspire the design of your new stadium?

Surprise Me

Chapters Two and Three discuss the design and construction of AT&T Stadium's two arches. After reading this book, what two or three facts about the arches surprised you? Write a few sentences about each fact. Why did you find each fact surprising?

Dig Deeper

After reading this book, what questions do you still have about AT&T Stadium? With an adult's help, find a few reliable sources that can help you answer your questions. Write a paragraph about what you learned.

Say What?

Reading about engineering challenges can mean learning a lot of new vocabulary. Find five words in this book that you had never heard before. Use a dictionary to find out what they mean. Then write the meanings in your own words. Use each word in a new sentence.

GLOSSARY

abutments
huge concrete support structures at the end of an arch

bolted
fastened together with a bolt and a nut

concrete
a building material made of cement, sand, gravel, and water

crane
a large machine used to lift and move heavy objects

ducts
large round pipes that carry air

end zone
one of the two ends of a football field

LED
light-emitting diode, a device that creates light using less electricity than traditional light bulbs

retractable
able to be opened and closed

scaffolds
platforms that workers stand on to reach high places

translucent
letting some light through

truss
a strong structure made of triangle shapes

LEARN
MORE

Books

Glave, Tom. *Dallas Cowboys*. Minneapolis, MN: Abdo Publishing, 2016.

Graham, Ian. *Amazing Stadiums*. Mankato, MN: Amicus, 2011.

Kaur, Ramandeep. *The Bird's Nest: How Did They Build That?* Fremont, CA: Scobre Press, 2015.

Websites

To learn more about Building by Design, visit **abdobooklinks.com**. These links are routinely monitored and updated to provide the most current information available.

Visit **abdocorelibrary.com** for free additional tools for teachers and students.

INDEX

About the Author

Barbara Lowell is the author of *George Ferris, What a
Wheel!, Daring Amelia*, and forthcoming books for children.
She lives in Tulsa, Oklahoma, not far from AT&T Stadium and
Tornado Alley.